Facts About Countries
Great Britain

Clare Oliver

SEA-TO-SEA
Mankato Collingwood London

This edition first published in 2009 by
Sea-to-Sea Publications
Distributed by Black Rabbit Books
P.O. Box 3263
Mankato, Minnesota 56002

Copyright © 2005, 2009 Bender Richardson White

Printed in China

All rights reserved.

Library of Congress
Cataloging-in-Publication Data:

Oliver, Clare.
  Great Britain / Clare Oliver.
     p. cm. -- (Facts about countries)
  Includes index.
  Summary: "Describes the geography, history, industries,
education, government, and cultures of Great Britain. Includes
maps, charts, and graphs"--Provided by publisher.
  ISBN 978-1-59771-116-6
  1. Great Britain--Juvenile literature. I. Title.
  DA27.5.O45 2009
  941--dc22
                                    2008004635

9 8 7 6 5 4 3 2

Published by arrangement with the Watts
Publishing Group Ltd, London.

Facts About Countries is produced for Franklin
Watts by Bender Richardson White, PO Box 266,
Uxbridge, UK.
Editor: Lionel Bender
Designer and Page Make-up: Ben White
Picture Researcher: Cathy Stastny
Cover Make-up: Mike Pilley, Radius
Production: Kim Richardson

Graphics and Maps: Stefan Chabluk
Educational Advisor: Prue Goodwin, Institute of
Education, The University of Reading
Consultant: Dr. Terry Jennings, a former
geography teacher and university lecturer. He is
now a full-time writer of children's geography and
science books.

Picture Credits

Pages: 1: PhotoDisc Inc./Jeremy Hoare. 3: PhotoDisc Inc./Andrew Ward/Life File. 4: PhotoDisc Inc/Colin Paterson. 6: Hutchison Photo Library/Robert Francis. 8: Hutchison Photo Library/Jeremy Horner. 9: Hutchison Photo Library/Peter Morzynski. 10 top: PhotoDisc Inc./Andrew Ward/Life File. 10-11 bottom: PhotoDisc Inc./Jeremy Hoare. 12 DAS Photo/David Simson. 14-15 bottom: Hutchison Photo Library. 16-17: Eye Ubiquitous/G. Daniels. 18 top: John Walmsley Photography. 18 bottom: Ted Spiegal/Corbis Images. 20: Hutchison Photo Library/Bernard Gérard. 21: Eye Ubiquitous/Martin Foyle. 22: Hutchison Photo Library/Bernard Gérard. 23: PhotoDisc Inc./Andrew Ward/Life File. 24: Peter Tumley/Corbis Images. 26 PhotoDisc Inc./Andrew Ward/Life File. 28: Reuters NewMedia Inc./Corbis Images. 29: Howard Davis/Corbis Images. 30: PhotoDisc Inc./John Wang. 31: PhotoDisc Inc./Andrew Ward/Life File. Cover photo: Digital Vision.

The Author

Clare Oliver is a full-time writer and editor of non-fiction books. She has written more than 50 books for children. This is her second book about Great Britain.

Note to parents and teachers

Every effort has been made by the Publishers to ensure that the websites in this book are suitable for children, that they are of the highest educational value, and that they contain no inappropriate or offensive material. However, because of the nature of the Internet, it is impossible to guarantee that the contents of these sites will not be altered. We strongly advise that Internet access is supervised by a responsible adult.

R0431119056

Contents

Welcome to Great Britain

Great Britain is made up of the kingdoms of England and Scotland and the principality of Wales. Together with the province of Northern Ireland, it is part of the United Kingdom (UK).

Worldwide influence

Great Britain was the first nation in the world to make its wealth from industry and manufacturing rather than farming. Despite being small, until the early 20th century Great Britain had a large empire. Today it is a member of the European Union (EU) and United Nations (UN) and still plays a important part in world events.

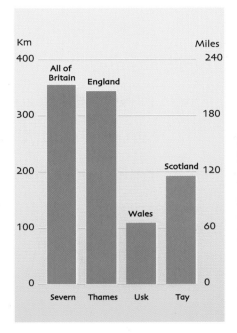

Above. The length of Britain's longest rivers. The Severn River runs through England and Wales.

Below. Many castles in Great Britain— like this one in Scotland—date back more than 400 years, before England, Scotland, and Wales were joined.

12°W 10°W 8°W 6°W 4°W 2°W 0° 2°E

Capital
Mountains
Country boundary

Major cities and towns
Grassland and farming

0 ——————— 150 Miles
0 ——————— 250 Kilometers

SHETLAND ISLANDS

Fair Isle

ORKNEY ISLANDS

Lewis

OUTER HEBRIDES

St. Kilda

Skye

Inverness

Fraserburgh
Peterhead

Spey

Don

Aberdeen

HIGHLANDS

Ben Nevis △

GRAMPIAN MTS.

Dee

Montrose

Mull

Oban

Tay

Dundee

Forth

Perth

ATLANTIC
OCEAN

Islay

Glasgow

Edinburgh

Holy I.

Ayr

Clyde

SCOTLAND

Tweed

Arran

NORTH
SEA

Stranraer

CHEVIOT HILLS

Newcastle upon Tyne

Carlisle

Tyne

Durham

LAKE
DISTRICT

PENNINES

Middlesbrough

NORTHERN
IRELAND

Lough
Neagh

Isle of
Man

Douglas

IRISH
SEA

Preston

Leeds

Hull

Liverpool

Manchester

The
Wash

REPUBLIC
OF
IRELAND

Holyhead

SNOWDONIA

Wrexham

Sheffield

Derby

Trent

Cardigan
Bay

Aberystwyth

ENGLAND

Wolverhampton

Norwich

Birmingham

Coventry

Peterborough

Cambridge

Northampton

Ipswich

WALES

Wye

Severn

COTSWOLD HILLS

Oxford

Colchester

Carmarthen

Usk

London

Swansea

Avon

Thames

Cardiff

Bristol

Canterbury

Bristol Channel

Salisbury

Brighton

Dover

Folkestone

Lundy

Southampton

Bournemouth

Isle of
Wight

Exeter

DARTMOOR

Plymouth

Penzance

ENGLISH CHANNEL

ISLES OF
SCILLY

Alderney

CHANNEL ISLANDS

Guernsey

FRANCE

Jersey

ST. GEORGE'S CHANNEL

N
W E
S

5

The Land

Britain's landscape varies from gentle hills to steep mountains. A mild, wet climate keeps much of the land fertile.

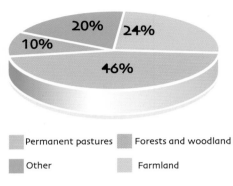

20% 24%
10%
46%

- Permanent pastures
- Other
- Forests and woodland
- Farmland

Above. **How land is used in Great Britain.**

Below. **Typical countryside in southern England.**

Rainfall

The wettest places are the highlands of Scotland, the Lake District, and Snowdonia. All of these get more than 12in (30cm) of rain each year. The east of Britain is much drier. Some places there get less than 3in (7cm) of rain in a year.

Landscape and temperature

The middle part of Scotland consists of low hills and is mostly farmland. Toward Scotland's border with England, the land rises. Northern England is rugged and bleak.

The Pennines are a chain of hills that run like a spine from northern England to the Midlands. Central and eastern England have mostly low plains. The Welsh landscape includes mountains in both the north and south.

The average annual temperature in Great Britain ranges from about 44°F (7°C) in the far north to about 52°F (11°C) on the Cornish coast in the southwest.

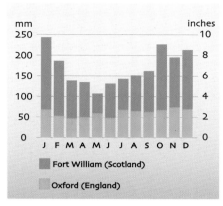

Above. **Rainfall each month in a town in Scotland and a town in England.**

Fort William (Scotland)

Oxford (England)

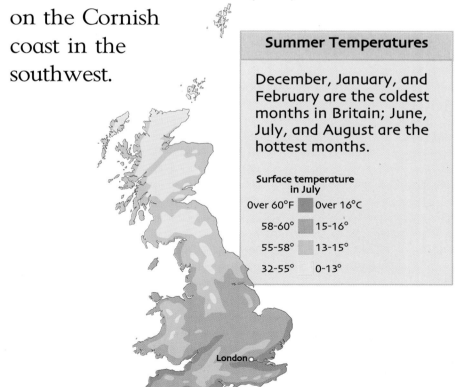

London

Summer Temperatures

December, January, and February are the coldest months in Britain; June, July, and August are the hottest months.

Surface temperature in July

Over 60°F	Over 16°C
58–60°	15–16°
55–58°	13–15°
32–55°	0–13°

Animal Life

Great Britain's mammals include deer, squirrels, moles, badgers, foxes, rabbits, hares, mice, voles, and bats. Among reptiles and amphibians are lizards, frogs, newts, and toads.
Birdlife includes several types of gulls, ducks, geese, chickadees, and swans as well as ptarmigan, golden eagles, and gray herons.

Web Search ►►

► www.met-office.gov.uk
Weather information from the Meteorological Office.

The People

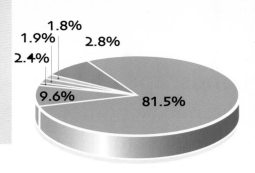

1.8%
1.9%
2.8%
2.4%
9.6%
81.5%

■ English ■ Scottish ■ Irish ■ Welsh
■ Ulster ■ West Indian, Indian, Pakistani, and Ot

Above. **The original nationalities of the people of Great Britain.**

As well as the native Scots, Welsh, and English, many other people have settled in Britain over the centuries.

Ancestors and language

The Scots and Welsh are descendants of the Celts, who settled the islands in prehistoric times. They now make up 12 percent of the population. The English are a mix of the German, Danish, and French people who arrived between about C.E. 400 and 1200.

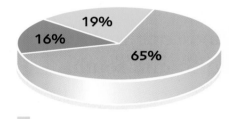

19%
16%
65%

■ 0-14 Total 11.2million (Men 5.8m/Women 5.5m)
■ 15-64 Total 38.5million (Men 19.4m/Women19.1m)
■ 65+ Total 9.2million (Men 3.8m/Women 15.4m)

Above. **Numbers of men and women. Men live to about 75 years of age and women to about 80.**

After World War II, people from former British colonies such as India, Hong Kong, and the West Indies were encouraged to come to Britain. They now make up 4.5 percent of the population.

The country's official language is English. About one-quarter of people in Wales speak Welsh. Scots Gaelic is spoken by about 60,000 people.

Right. **At Speakers' Corner in London, people of any nationality, culture, or religion can speak openly.**

Below. **Immigrants granted British citizenship in 2000.**

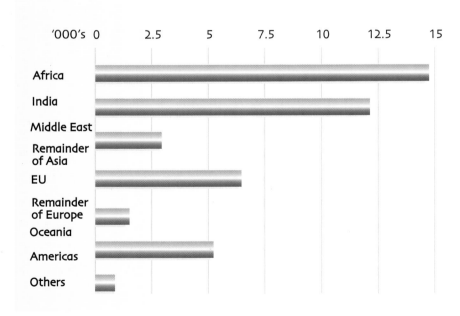

| '000's | 0 | 2.5 | 5 | 7.5 | 10 | 12.5 | 15 |

Africa
India
Middle East
Remainder of Asia
EU
Remainder of Europe
Oceania
Americas
Others

Above. **Most British people live in the southeast of England. They travel to work by train, bus, and car.**

Web Search ▶▶

▶ www.statistics.gov.uk
Up-to-the-minute facts and figures about Great Britain and the United Kingdom.

▶ www.direct.gov.uk/Home page/fs/en
▶ www.wales.gov.uk
▶ www.scotland.gov.uk/
▶ www.discovernorthern ireland.com
Information on all parts of Britain and the United Kingdom.

Above. In the countryside, there are small cottages like these, as well as large country houses like the one shown on page 6.

Population Density

Great Britain has one of the world's highest numbers of people per square mile.

Population–people per sq. mile/km

2,600 or over	1,000 or over
1,500-2,600	600-999
780-1,500	300-599
390-780	150-299
under 390	under 150

Edinburgh

Manchester

Birmingham

Cardiff

London

Right. Traffic in London. London is the largest city in Great Britain with more than seven million people.

Town and Country Life

More than 90 percent of British people live in towns and cities. The country is twice as crowded as its neighbor France.

Houses, shops, and offices

Many people have moved to the countryside and travel into cities to work. As a result, new houses and shopping areas have grown around villages. In industrial cities built in the late 1800s you can still see rows of red-brick houses.

During the 1950s and 1960s, the local government built apartments to fill areas destroyed by bombing in World War II. More recently, private homes have been built in the suburbs and in growing towns such as East Kilbride and Milton Keynes.

In the last 10 years, new houses, offices, and shopping malls have been built in the rundown docklands of major cities, including London, Liverpool, and Edinburgh.

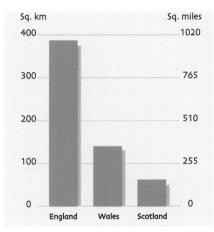

Above. **Population density (people per square mile).**

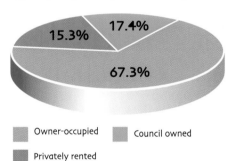

17.4%

15.3%

67.3%

Owner-occupied   Council owned

Privately rented

Above. **People who own or rent their houses.**

Web Search ▶▶

▶ **www.streetmap.co.uk**
Find and print a street map of any British town or village.

▶ **http://www.dsdni.gov.uk/index/hsdiv-housing.htm**
Facts and figures about houses and homes in Britain.

11

Farming and Fishing

DATABASE

Freshwater fishing

Today, most inland fishing is done for sport, not to catch fish to sell. But there are also salmon and trout farms, mostly in Scotland.

Freshwater catches include salmon, trout, roach, perch, carp, freshwater eel, pike, and grayling.

Below. **A small fishing boat in a harbor.**

Low-lying land is mostly used to grow crops. Hills are used for grazing animals.

Crops and livestock

Britain's main crops are cereal crops (wheat, barley, and oats), canola, sugarbeet, and potatoes. Fruit and vegetables are grown in southeastern England.

Sheep and cattle are the most important livestock, followed by pigs and poultry. Wales is famous for its lamb and Scotland for its beef. Dairy products include milk, butter, and cheese.

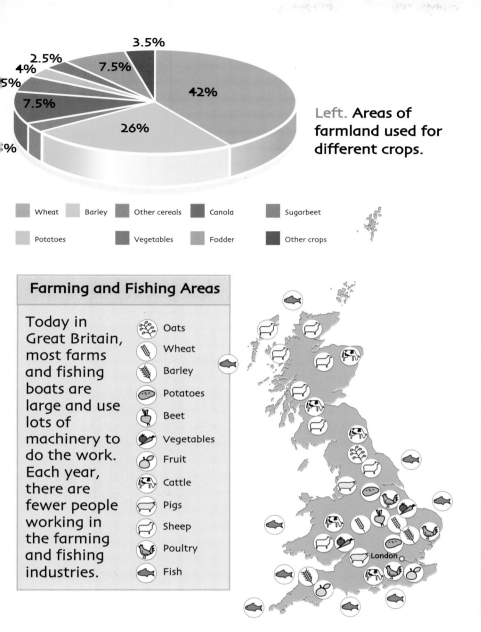

Left. Areas of farmland used for different crops.

3.5%
2.5%
4%
5%
7.5%
7.5%
42%
26%
%

- Wheat
- Barley
- Other cereals
- Canola
- Sugarbeet
- Potatoes
- Vegetables
- Fodder
- Other crops

Farming and Fishing Areas

Today in Great Britain, most farms and fishing boats are large and use lots of machinery to do the work. Each year, there are fewer people working in the farming and fishing industries.

- Oats
- Wheat
- Barley
- Potatoes
- Beet
- Vegetables
- Fruit
- Cattle
- Pigs
- Sheep
- Poultry
- Fish

London

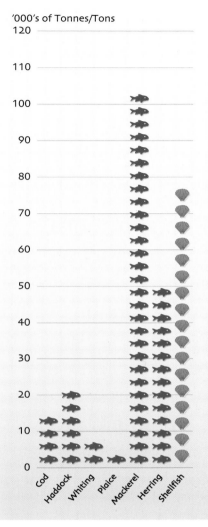

'000's of Tonnes/Tons

120
110
100
90
80
70
60
50
40
30
20
10
0

Cod | Haddock | Whiting | Plaice | Mackerel | Herring | Shellfish

Above. Fish catches per year made by Great Britain's sea-going fishing boats.

The fishing industry

There are more than 8,000 fishing boats in Britain. They catch more than 660,000 tons of seafish a year, more than 65 percent of the country's needs. Overfishing has reduced the numbers of fish caught, but an area in the North Sea known as the Dogger Bank remains one of the world's richest fishing grounds.

Web Search ►►

► www.defra.gov.uk/
Information about farming and fishing from the Department for Environment Food and Rural Affairs.

Resources and Industry

Great Britain is one of the world's top industrial countries. About 20 percent of people work in manufacturing, creating one-quarter of the country's wealth.

Fuels, minerals, and products

Britain produces 110 million tons of coal each year. Most of this coal is burned in power stations. With oil and gas in the North Sea, Britain has more energy resources than any other EU country. Its mineral resources include tin and zinc.

   The main products of Britain's factories are electronics, cars, aircraft, chemicals, synthetic fibers, foods, and plastics.

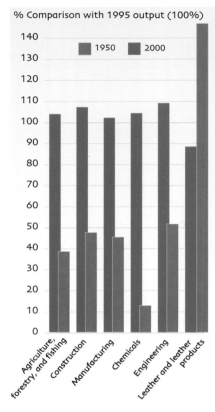

% Comparison with 1995 output (100%)

■ 1950   ■ 2000

Agriculture, forestry, and fishing; Construction; Manufacturing; Chemicals; Engineering; Leather and leather products

Above. **Rise and fall of the output of selected industries.**

All kinds of services

Of all workers, 65 percent work in the service industries. They have jobs selling goods or giving help, advice, and support. Examples of service industries are tourism, banking, computing, and insurance. The number of shops, restaurants, gyms, and banks grows each year.

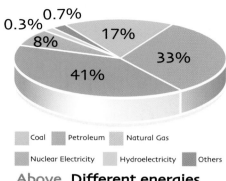

0.3% 0.7%
8% 17%
41% 33%

Coal Petroleum Natural Gas
Nuclear Electricity Hydroelectricity Others

Above. **Different energies used in 2000.**

Fossil Fuels and Industry

Fossil fuels—coal, oil, and natural gas—are found in the north and off the coast. Most factories are found in the Midlands and northeast. Service industries are found mostly in the southeast.

Oil
Gas
Coal

North Sea Oil and Gas fields

London

Left. **Oil rigs built in Scotland, ready to be moved to oil fields in the North Sea.**

Major changes

Since 1975, Britain's output of crude oil has increased 80 times, output of natural gas and nuclear electricity have trebled, while coal production has more than halved.

Today, Britain uses only 10 percent more energy than it did in 1975. However, the industrial output has doubled. This is because its use of energy is far more efficient. Also, Britain's power stations produce far less pollution than they did in 1975.

Web Search ►►

► http://www.berr.gov.uk/publications/index.html
The UK Department of Trade and Industry website.

15

Transportation

Britain's main transportation routes are roads and highways. There is also a big railroad network, and airlines fly to most parts of the country.

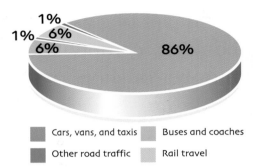

1%
1%
6%
6%
86%

- Cars, vans, and taxis
- Buses and coaches
- Other road traffic
- Rail travel
- Internal flights

Above. **Travelers using each type of transportation.**

Road and rail

In the 1900s, most goods were transported by trains and canal barges. Trucks now carry 65 percent of goods. The biggest users of the road are car drivers. Some people travel to work by train. Others use buses, motorcycles, and bicycles.

Below. **Britain has 27.5 million registered road vehicles. Traffic jams are a common problem.**

Highway Links

The major highways run north-south, to Wales, and between Liverpool, Manchester, and Leeds. The M25 opened in 1986. It is a circular highway that allows heavy traffic to bypass the busy center of London.

Edinburgh

Manchester

Birmingham

Cardiff

London

M25

Motorways

Air and sea routes

Air traffic in Britain has increased a lot in recent years, and there are international airports in many British cities.

Cargo leaves and enters Britain mainly by ship. Ferries from Dover carry passengers to mainland Europe. Increasingly, though, cargo and passengers travel to mainland Europe by train through the Channel Tunnel, which links Britain and France.

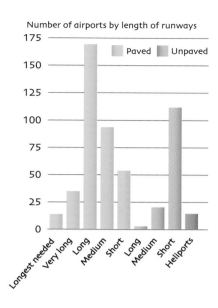

Number of airports by length of runways

Paved   Unpaved

Longest needed, Very long, Long, Medium, Short, Long, Medium, Short, Heliports

Above. **Britain's airports and heliports. Heathrow is Europe's busiest airport**

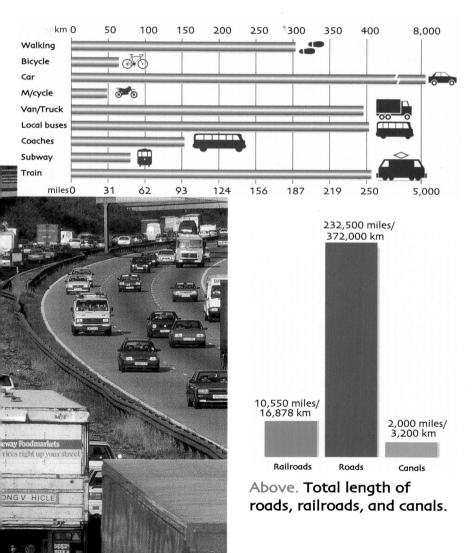

Left. **Average distances people travel in a year by the main types of transportation.**

Above. **Total length of roads, railroads, and canals.**

232,500 miles/ 372,000 km

10,550 miles/ 16,878 km

2,000 miles/ 3,200 km

Railroads   Roads   Canals

Web Search ►►

► www.rail.co.uk
Railroad companies, their timetables, and travel services.

► www.theaa.co.uk
The Automobile Association.

► www.caa.co.uk
The Civil Aviation Authority.

► www.abports.co.uk
The Association of British Ports.

Above. In many secondary schools, students must wear a uniform.

Left. Cambridge University is one of the oldest universities in Britain. It dates from the thirteenth century.

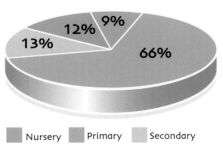

Nursery   Primary   Secondary

Colleges

9%

12%

13%

66%

Above. Number of schools at all levels.

Education

British children must go to school between the ages of five and 16. Education is free but some children go to private, fee-paying schools.

From nursery to university

Many children go to nursery school from the age of three. When they are five, children start primary school. Here they are taught mostly reading, writing, and math skills. There is a national curriculum for England and Wales. This means that schools teach the same subjects to the same levels of difficulty. Scotland has its own, similar system.

Most children over the age of 11 study a range of subjects at secondary school. Then, at age 14 or 15, they start to study for exams called GCSEs, or SSGs in Scotland. Children may then leave school or go to college to study further.

Students gain a university place based on their exam results. Many people get student loans to pay for their studies. Sometimes they receive money from the government.

DATABASE

TV Education
The Open University was set up in 1971. Its students do not go to classes, so they can study and have a job at the same time. Television and radio programs back up the course work.

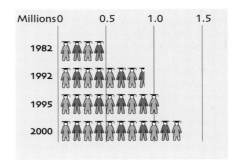

Above. **Growth in the number of students who go to university.**

Web Search ►►

► www.dfes.gov.uk
Information from Britain's Department for Education and Skills.

Sports and Leisure

Top Sports

Sports most commonly played at British schools are, in order:
1. Athletics—35 percent of students
2. Gymnastics—33 percent
3. Rounders (similar to baseball)—31 percent
4. Swimming—30 percent
5. Soccer—28 percent

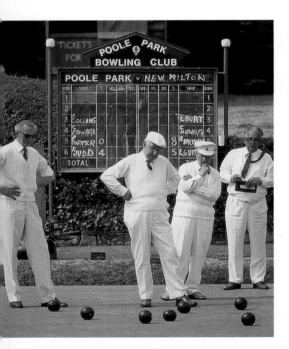

Above. **Bowls is a traditional British sport. It is played both indoors and outdoors.**

Many of the world's most popular sports began in Britain, including soccer, rugby, golf, tennis, and cricket.

Teams, clubs, and competitions

To many, soccer is Britain's national sport. Teams such as Manchester United, Chelsea, Arsenal, and Liverpool are world famous.

Rugby originated at Rugby School in Warwickshire. Today, there are two versions of the game: rugby league and rugby union. Rugby league is played mainly in northern England. England, Scotland, and Wales play rugby union at an international level. In 2003, England won the rugby union World Cup.

Scotland is the home of golf and England is the home of tennis and cricket. The most important golf club is St. Andrews near Dundee. The world's most famous tennis club, in Wimbledon, southwest London, hosts a major tennis tournament every summer. Cricket is played throughout England. Internationals, called test matches, are played in the summer. Cricket is also played in the south of Wales.

Above. Soccer internationals are played at larger stadiums across the country, including the Millennium Stadium in Cardiff, Wales, shown here.

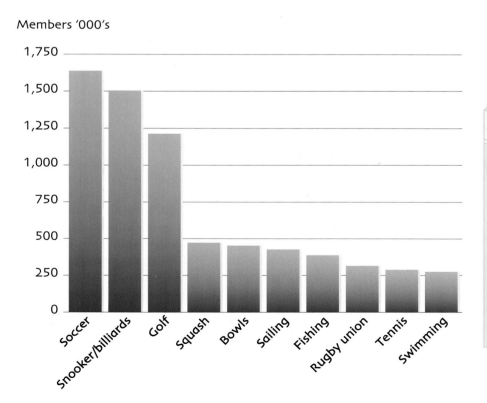

Members '000's

Left. The number of people belonging to sports clubs.

Web Search ►►

► www.culture.gov.uk
Government department for Culture, Media and Sport.

► www.sportengland.org
► www.ssc.org.uk
► www.sports-council-wales.
  co.uk
The sports organizations of England, Scotland, and Wales.

Daily Life and Religion

In Britain, people usually go to school from Monday to Friday and work from 9 A.M. to 5:30 P.M. each day.

Relaxing and shopping

Watching TV and listening to the radio are the main forms of relaxation. Shopping is a popular weekend activity. People shop at local markets or in large shopping centers.

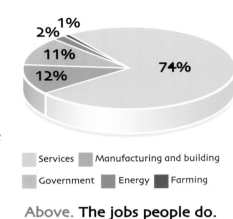

2% 1%
11%
12%
74%

Services   Manufacturing and building
Government   Energy   Farming

Above. **The jobs people do.**

Below. **A typical street market.**

22

Religion and health care

Most people in Britain are Christians. The Anglican Church is the state religion. Other Christian groups include Roman Catholics, Methodists, Presbyterians, and Baptists. Britain has the second-largest Jewish community in Europe and growing communities of Muslims, Hindus, and Sikhs.

Public healthcare is provided by the National Health Service (NHS). People can visit doctors, dentists, and opticians and also receive free hospital treatment. There are also private hospitals and doctors.

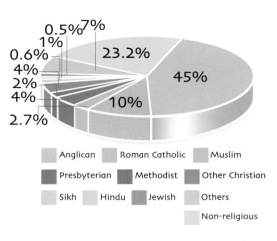

Above. **Percentages of people belonging to religions.**

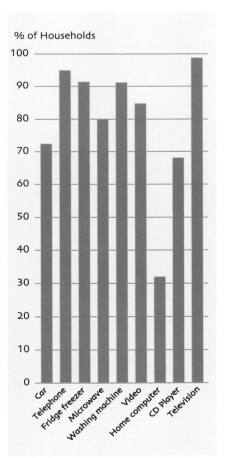

Above. **Electrical goods owned by people in Britain.**

Above. **Towns such as Winchester, in England, are built around a historic cathedral.**

23

Arts and Media

Britain produces newspapers, books, plays, movies, and television programs. It also has world-famous galleries and museums and specialist art collections.

Theater, music, and dance

London's West End is called "theaterland." The Cardiff and Edinburgh Festivals are two major events that take place each year. They are celebrations of dance, music, and literature.

Below. **A street performer at the Edinburgh Festival.**

Web Search ▶▶

▶ **www.visitbritain.com/** Links to all Britain's tourist attractions.

▶ **www.resource.gov.uk** Britain's museum website.

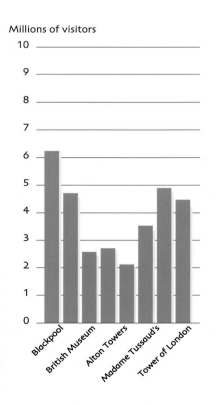

Millions of copies

Above. More people in Britain read newpapers than anywhere else in the world.

Millions of visitors

Left. Millions of people visit Britain's tourist attractions.

Movies, literature, newspapers

The movie industry in Britain is booming. Many movies have been based on the works of British writers such as William Shakespeare and Charles Dickens.

The British Broadcasting Corporation (BBC) broadcasts two main television channels and five national radio stations. Channel 4, Channel 5, and ITV are independent television channels. Viewers can also watch satellite and cable television programs from around the world. There are also many radio stations.

The most famous British newspapers are *The Times, The Mirror, The Sun,* and *The Guardian.* The biggest-selling regional paper is the *Glasgow Daily Record.*

▭ ░░░░░░ **DATABASE** ░░░░░░

Famous Arts Institutions
• Birmingham Philharmonic Orchestra
• English National Opera
• Royal Ballet Company
• Royal Shakespeare Company
• Scottish Opera
• National Eisteddfod Society

Museums and Galleries
• Ashmolean Museum, Oxford
• British Museum, London
• Museum of Scotland, Edinburgh
• National Museum of Wales, Cardiff
• Tate Modern, London
• Tate, Liverpool
• Victoria and Albert Museum, London

Government

The queen is officially the head of state but Great Britain is actually governed by parliament. Members of Parliament (MPs) are elected by the British people.

Elections and parliaments

Elections are held once every five years, or sometimes more often. Everyone aged 18 or over may vote in elections.

Elected MPs sit in the House of Commons in London. Most MPs belong to the Conservative, Labour, or Liberal Democratic Parties. The party that has the most MPs after an election forms a government. This is led by the Cabinet, which is made up of a team of between 10 and 30 MPs and the prime minister, the leader of the ruling party.

British people also elect members to the European Parliament based in Brussels.

Below. The clock tower of the Houses of Parliament. There is also a Scottish Parliament and Welsh and Northern Ireland Assemblies. They deal with regional issues.

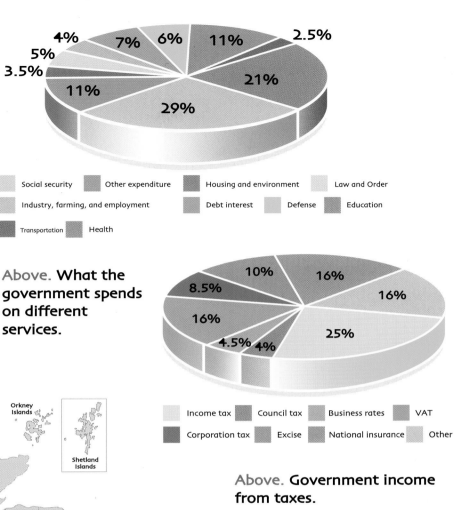

Social security	Other expenditure	Housing and environment	Law and Order
Industry, farming, and employment	Debt interest	Defense	Education
Transportation	Health		

Above. **What the government spends on different services.**

Income tax	Council tax	Business rates	VAT
Corporation tax	Excise	National insurance	Other

Above. **Government income from taxes.**

In Parliament

Decisions are made by a majority vote in parliament. There are two divisions, or "houses," in parliament. Proposals, or Bills, are put to the House of Commons for MPs to vote on. Bills then go before the House of Lords. The Lords often suggest changes and these are usually added in. When a Bill has been voted for and agreed, it becomes an Act of Parliament and a law.

Local Government

Britain is divided into counties. The counties are each split into several boroughs. Each borough has its own council of locally elected members.

Major Counties

Other Authorities

Web Search ▶▶

▶ www.explore.parliament.uk
Introduction to the British parliament.

▶ www.royal.gov.uk
The official website of the British monarchy.

▶ www.scottish.parliament.uk/ home.htm
Website of Scotland's Parliament.

▶ www.number-10.gov.uk
Features the history of the prime minister's home at No.10 Downing Street.

27

DATABASE

Important dates

C.E. 43 The Romans invade Britain

500s Angles, Saxons, and Jutes settle

789 Viking raids

1066 Norman Conquest

1536 England and Wales formally united

1601 James VI of Scotland inherits English throne from Elizabeth I and becomes King James I

1640s English Civil War

1707 Act of Union between Scotland and England

1776 United States gains independence from Britain

1780s–1800s Industrial Revolution

1801 Ireland made part of the United Kingdom

1922 Republic of Ireland gains independence

1999 Welsh National Assembly and Scottish Parliament formed

Place in the World

In 1900, Great Britain had a huge empire. It had colonies all over the world. By 1970, most of its territories abroad were independent. Today, Great Britain is still a world power.

War and peace

In 1931, the British Empire became the Commonwealth. After World War II, it helped set up the United Nations. The UN's purpose is to maintain world peace.

Below. **Members of the British Royal Family in 2000, including Queen Elizabeth II and the Queen Mother (center, who died in 2002), and Prince Charles (second from right).**

Below. **Oxfam, a British aid relief charity, works with NATO forces in Kosovo.**

NATO and the EU

In 1949, Great Britain also founded the North Atlantic Treaty Organization (NATO), a military agreement with the United States and several European countries. In 1973, it joined the European Economic Community, which has since become the European Union (EU). This allows tourists, students, and workers to travel and work between EU countries.

Although half of Britain's trade is with other EU countries, the United States is its single biggest trading partner. Many British people think of themselves as separate and different from continental Europeans.

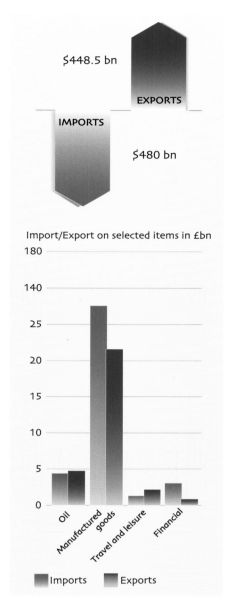

$448.5 bn

EXPORTS

IMPORTS

$480 bn

Import/Export on selected items in £bn

180

140

25

20

15

10

5

0

Oil   Manufactured goods   Travel and leisure   Financial

■ Imports   ■ Exports

Above. **Major imports and exports.**

🌐 **Web Search ▶▶**

▶ www.nationalarchives.gov. uk/
The National Archives, which holds government and public documents.

▲ **Stonehenge, a prehistoric circle of stones in England.**

Area:
88,800 sq miles (229,991 sq km)

Population size:
57,133,900

Capital city:
London (population 7,074,300)

Longest river:
Severn (220 miles/354 km)

Highest mountain:
Ben Nevis (4,406ft/1,343 m)

Largest lake:
Loch Lomond (24 sq miles/71 sq km)

Flag:
The UK's national flag is the Union Jack, which combines the crosses of St. George of England (red cross on white background), St. Andrew of Scotland (diagonal white cross on blue), and St. Patrick of Ireland (diagonal red cross on white). The Welsh flag features a red dragon on a green and white background.

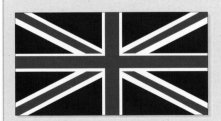

Official language:
English

Currency:
Pound sterling (£)

Major resources:
Oil, gas, coal, tin, limestone, iron ore, salt, clay, chalk, gypsum, lead, silica

Major exports:
Manufactured goods, fuels, machinery, chemicals, transportation equipment, financial services

National holidays and special events:
New Year's Day (January 1)
St. David's Day (March 1)
Oxford vs. Cambridge University Boat Race (last week in March)
Good Friday, Easter Sunday, and Easter Monday (March or April)
St. George's Day (April 23)
Early May Bank Holiday (first Monday in May)
Spring Bank Holiday (last Monday in May)
Queen's official birthday (June)
Edinburgh Festival (August)
Summer Bank Holiday (August)
Guy Fawkes' Day (November 5)
Remembrance Day (Sunday nearest November 11)
St. Andrew's Day (November 30)
Christmas Day (December 25)
Boxing Day (December 26)
New Year's Eve/Hogmanay (December 31)

Religions:
Anglican, Roman Catholic, Muslim, Presbyterian, Methodist, Sikh, Hindu, Jewish

Key Words

CLIMATE
The range of weather in a region over time.

COLONY
An area of land that is taken over, settled, and ruled by another country.

COMMONWEALTH
A group of independent countries that were once part of the British Empire.

DOCKLANDS
An area in a city along a major river that was once the main port used by ships.

EMPIRE
A group of colonies ruled by a single country.

EXPORTS
Goods sold to a foreign country.

FERTILE
Land suitable for growing crops.

GOVERNMENT
The group of people who manage the country, deciding on its laws, raising taxes, and organizing health, industry, farming, education, transportation, and other national systems and services.

GRAZING
Feeding on grass and shrubs in fields and open areas.

HYDROELECTRIC ITY
Electrical power created from flowing water.

IMMIGRANTS
People who come from one country to live in another.

IMPORTS
Goods bought from a foreign country.

KINGDOM
A territory ruled by a king or queen.

LIVESTOCK
Animals that are raised on a farm for their meat, milk, wool, and skins.

MANUFACTURING
Using machinery to make products from raw materials.

NATIONAL CURRICULUM
The government plan for teaching, learning, and testing subjects in schools.

NUCLEAR ELECTRICITY
Electricity produced by splitting atoms of uranium to release heat energy.

PARLIAMENT
A seat of government. The UK parliament is divided into the House of Commons and the House of Lords.

POLLUTION
Damage to the environment.

POPULATION DENSITY
The average number of people living on a particular area of land.

PRINCIPALITY
A territory controlled by a prince (in the same way that a kingdom is controlled by a king or queen).

PROVINCE
A part of a country or state that has a certain identity.

RESOURCES
A country's supplies of energy, natural materials, and minerals.

Index